LEAVING THE ISLAND

Leaving the Island

TALYA RUBIN

Signal
EDITIONS

THE POETRY IMPRINT AT VÉHICULE PRESS

Published with the generous assistance of The Canada Council for the
Arts and the Canada Book Fund of the Department of Canadian Heritage,
and the Société de développement des entreprises culturelles du Québec
(SODEC)

Signal Editions Editor: Carmine Starnino

Cover design: David Drummond
Photo of author: Terry Hughes
Set in Filosofia and Minion by Simon Garamond
Printed by Marquis Book Printing Inc.

Dépôt légal, Library and Archives Canada and the
Bibliothèque national du Québec, secondtrimester 2015.

Library and Archives Canada Cataloguing in Publication

Rubin, Talya, author
Leaving the island / Talya Rubin.

Poems.
Issued in print and electronic formats.
isbn 978-1-55065-403-5 (pbk.).– isbn 978-1-55065-412-7 (epub)

I. Title.

ps8635.u296l42 2015   c811'.6   c2014-908336-x
C2014-908337-8

Published by Véhicule Press, Montréal, Québec, Canada
www.vehiculepress.com

Distribution in Canada by LitDistCo
www.litdistco.ca

Distributed in the U.S. by Independent Publishers Group
www.ipgbook.com

Printed in Canada on FSC® certified paper.

*To my husband, Nick, who continues to believe
and be a light in any kind of darkness.*

*To my son, Misha, who let me write when all he really
wanted was milk.*

And to my mum and dad, the originators of all this.

Contents

St Kilda, Scotland

"No fort of trees, not even the least shrub grows here, nor has a bee ever been seen."

–Martin Martin, *A Late Voyage to St Kilda* (1698)

Leaving the Island

We've all gone now, left the place to the sheep
and the gannet, the puffin and the wren.

For decades only a mailboat of whalebone and oak
came and went from here. Then the tourists

arrived to see if we were more than myth in the Outer
Hebrides. We sold them tweed and spotted

bird's eggs, let them look in on prayer meetings, count
the stones in the walls we built to keep out the weather.

When we prayed it was for a cease
to things: the wind, the war, the plagues.

In the end, the land choked us out, carcasses
of sea birds and layers of peat moss turned to lead

the constant fog, the solitude, the slippery grass
by the cliff's edge, that impossible winter of 1929.

We left our Bibles open and handfuls of oats on the floor.
Locked our doors behind us. From this vantage point

our home was just a sketch of land that shrank into the sea—
the island's sharp crags impossible to understand.

This land, so angry and so peaceful now, without
us. The feral sheep bleat into the evening.

Nothing to bother them but old age and the wind
that made us all walk like bent trees.

The Puffin Catchers

I imagine the women in black hoop skirts
the structures made of fulmar bone
billowing up the craggy rock.

There is nothing to collect here
no bounty, no possibility
only the seabirds.

And so they go these groups of women
abseiling down cliffs
with horsehair ropes.

Or landing boats on impossible
shores of some other island
even more remote than this one.

To scare the puffins from their holes
in turf where they huddle with their young
the women bring their dogs along.

They almost look like landed
British gentry and this their hunting
sport. But this is not a game

at all. The ropes of hair are laid
across the ground, a stone
at each end to weigh them down

a loop, a noose awaits
the web-footed odd-billed
flurry to emerge, trip up

and fall. They spend weeks like this
each day waiting for their prey
to land in traps, 300 or 400

downed by nightfall. Until, so exhausted
by their kill, the women fall to sleep
all in a row in huts built just for them.

The entrance to their narrow homes
so small, so low they need to crawl
on hands and knees to burrow in at night.

Nothing to lure them out but the promise
of dawn and birds to trap. The women
bring their Gaelic bibles, sleep in their clothes

lull themselves with words
of wonder and horror, the awe of life and death
is all they murmur in the candlelight.

A Total Absence of Trees

The mountains rise rugged, entirely bare
not a single tree will grow here.

The lakes are dark and reluctant
only clouds on their silver surface

in constant changeable shifts.
Light moves and wind moves

all else is fixed. This slate of
land serves as a canvas

to weather, the gods of high and lonely
places swoop down their moods

so that only these singular, remote humans
can witness their range of whim and folly.

But it is the wild fowl who truly see
here. From above, what looks like a great

grey mass, hides a verdant valley covered
(in spring) with buttercups, sea pinks and milk

white clover. The miracle of relentless rain
is this rare bucolic green.

There are springs, there are valleys, sheep
graze unfazed by the beating sea.

One hundred feet below boats flail
crazy in whirlpools of water

no landing place, no foothold
only slippery rock and seaweed.

No tree to cut to build a boat, a chair, a bed
peat and straw instead and mud and rock

and sea and salt and oily smell
of fish and fowl is all, all.

This howling wilderness
almost pastoral.

The Last Great Auk

The Auk so black they thought she was a witch.
A bringer of bad storms, a spirit gone wrong.

Flightless and uncertain she stood black beaked
and splendid, edging on extinction

one webbed foot at a time. No one knew her—
her name, her song, her habits. One egg a year

was all the Auk would lay. Not much bounty
to collect. The egg itself a spinning top

designed to waver at the edge of cliffs
and not fall off.

She couldn't go anywhere very fast,
except into the trap of a fowling rod.

They thought she'd come to steal the souls
of their already weakened babies.

They didn't know she was the last one
never to be seen after this day in July.

Roasted over a peat fire, an omen
to the extinction they soon faced, themselves.

How to Read the Weather

Here it is the wind and clouds that measure time
where the sun falls on this rock or this valley.
This shadow across this hill means noon—
chasing sheep or spinning wool
or a return to peat fires that
burn without cease.

The waves give signs of storm no matter what
the sky reads above. High breakers
at the eastern point—a rainstorm is about to hit.
When the sea crests white a squall is near despite
how bright the sun's gleam on tips of ocean masts.

The doors of the houses face northeast
to protect from southwest winds.
The thatch on roofs is tied down
to stone, so as not to blow away.

Here the animals all are speckled:
Stone Age sheep with enormous horns
the fowls, the seals, the eggs even,
all motley from this strange place.

So many fish crowd the sea:
cod, ling, mackerel, turbot
graylords, sythes
laiths, podloes, herring.

So many birds crowd the sky:
hawk, eagle, plover, wren
stone-chalker, cracker, cuckoo
geese, gairfowl, fulmar, scraber

bowger, razor-bill, sea-mall.
Although the cuckoo is only seen
when someone important dies.

Navigating by the Birds

The sky is white with gannets.
When the heavens are not clear it is the birds we steer by.

No compass will do—what are they to us
anyway? Needles bob behind glass, men squint, helpless

at the sea's splintering rage. Here birds glide and soar
they know the world as nothing but their own.

Why try to read the signs when they are everywhere?
We can't see the sun for the wingspan, for the bird

beat, for the flocks fissure overhead, cutting the world in two
earth and sky, sea and sky, all opposites, no bleed of blue into blue.

So many birds, they fall from above in argument over a nest
whose egg is whose, tufts of grass stolen from under

a peat fire gone out. It's that easy. They knock into one another
and we are ready to catch them when they do.

This promise: a bird from the sky into our open hands.

Mischevious Rock

The world is dizzy from the top.
They draw lots for Stackdonn, that tricky rock
has shaken more than a few men from its incline
it soars like a steeple to the height of the birds.

Up here you can touch a wing tip, plunge into the
wild fury of their squawk, pluck a feather with your teeth
as you balance on a thumb, legs swung outwards
into thin air, a sheer drop below, where bird
excrement tints the water an oily white and grey slick.

Sure, there's a rope around your midriff tied back
to the boat, where tiny men look like dolls made of wood
in a matchbox. They urge you on from this deafening
height, but all you hear are bird calls and the wind
and some occasional cry of congratulation
gulped into the insubstantial.

For all this you get four fowls assigned
to your family over and above your
portion. Four birds extra, and a reputation.
A hero of sorts, for surviving at all.

After the Solan Geese

To think you slender necked majestic birds, mythical white,
were worn as shoes. Split open at the seam and tender female feet

urged in to keep the damp and mud at bay; slippers of a sort.
The only plunge you made a final one into the thud of earth

not the dive of arrows into the sea your sharp beaks
once made, a weapon for the abundant fish.

The sky so thick with gannet you resemble white ash
not birds that rise above the rock and fog.

Coupling pairs with yellow-crested heads dusted with pigment,
a solid crown, your skulls resistant to impact from impossible heights.

The only way to catch is from above. The fish are all your bounty here,
herring swallowed by the beak-full, under water.

Sea-bound boats bob and flail in winds too fierce
for any fisherman's hook or line.

So they net you instead. From horsehair ropes bound with
the lining of sheep gut to keep from splitting off.

Men suspend themselves and poach you from your sea stack nests
dangle from cliff faces, their only implement a long stick

with a noose at the end to scoop you by the neck and snap it there
above the depths.

The goose-neck footwear only lasts four days, if that, then
tossed aside to sink into the ground, skin and carcass as mulch for crops.

Fowling

The sleeping geese too tired to cry out are knocked on the head
by the fowling crowd. 16,000 eggs consumed in a year, 22,000 birds.

Almost nothing grows here, you see? Astringent raw eggs that give strangers gas
a delicacy. This land is a compost of ash, urine, bone, straw.

How many carcasses dangle limp in drying houses? Beehive shaped cleits
the only industry here. Stone huts preserve the bodies, let the air through.

The birds come to gather grass for their nests and when they stop to rest
they are a startled target for the birders collecting to feed mouths.

No salt to preserve with, so birds are slit down their backs, laid out
to dry. Eggs are nestled in burnt turf ash to keep for months.

Fulmars scooped from rocks are taken by surprise from behind.
They vomit bellies full of oil from the fear.

Place a wick down a slicked throat for a bird lamp ready made. Such ingenuity
in the kill here. Only burnt ash and pickled bird and rotten eggs for food.

The fowlers catch their birds by night, while an entire flock is sleeping,
creep up in socks sewn of rag, with feathers as fasteners instead of thread.

These men almost birds themselves, and in the dreams of gannets could be
taken for a giant of their kind. One bird sits watch, cries out in panic and the whole

flock takes wing. 5,000 birds lost with one foot placed too firm on the rock,
a shadow cast too long, the moon too full. All that effort gone to waste.

Or else, success! Birds all hammered on the head and thrown down to sea bodies gather, shimmer white on the surface, until the boat men cry:

"Enough." So swamped with death they are. The dangle of bird necks, those transluscent eyes that seem to see the same forever, alive or dead.

9 Months Stranded on Harris

From the rocks of this island
we can see the other shore.

Breathless
we wait for the wind to stop.

Where I stand I can almost
make out a figure on the hillside

across.
But can I? Is it a man or a rock?

So sick of trying to understand time
the way growing old has nothing to do

with growing up.

I pluck hairs from my own head now
like the birds I once worked over

with my fingers. Balding, I mourn my former life.
All I want to do is get home.

Throw myself
into the sea no matter how torrid or how angry.

If only I could make myself small
fit into a mailboat

bob
in the bladder of a sheep

send some part of myself
to the other shore.

It feels like eternity is happening
every time I blink my eyes.

How can weather be
so cruel?

We only came to catch some birds,
some fish, three days worth of clothes

and home again to you, to all of you.

The longing I feel for my own island
is inscribed inside my chest.

The shape of the land carved there.
I want to tear it out of my heart

hold it in my palm, beating
like a fallen bird

I want to curl up against it
a broken thing

resting in its shape.

Plucking

I am eating feathers. Spit out their ticklish sprouts
between my teeth. Feathers in my hair and in my lungs.

Nothing to do but pluck the white translucent spines
each lined with soft layers I run my fingers through.

We would tease bare arms with this levity if there weren't
so many. This beauty and bounty like a plague

rising cloud of ghost birds storm the air.
Tarred and feathered the whole town is covered

in a shower of white and grey and black flecks
dusting us all like dirty snow, even the sheep

are decorated with them, a second coat. The interior white too,
mossy green carpet covered, and lilacs and bluebells and orchids

the only things to remind us of the season. Expectant mothers
with swollen bellies are graced with a feathery halo like a nest egg

about to break open. Their own bald babies will no doubt
resemble the awkward chicks, damp with downy fur.

The smell of roast puffin fills the air from every house
an ancient fish-like smell.

Feathers in our noses and the smell of charred flesh soaked
into our skin.

We make our way through summer like this
one bird at a time.

Known Land

These are cliffs for throwing oneself off of
my mother said madness ran
in the family.

We bury babies out at sea
mother's milk run dry
a rattle of dead birds and the suckling
of bones, hardly a substitute.

This is a place for dying. The smoke
from peat fires chokes our
young, the songs we sing so old
they roll around our lungs
like disease.

We are insignificant here. Forgotten.
I want to send a message
in a mailboat with only my
name on it.

In hope that someone somewhere
in the world will know me.
Isn't that why we live, to be known?

If there is a door in these stone
walls, let me at it
let me at it.
The imagined or the real
it doesn't matter
anymore.

Voyage to Australia, 1852

(In which 18 of 36 St Kildans died at sea)

Anywhere is closer to home than here
The horizon is endless and flat
As soon as you leave, your land is near
The light you remember, where you once sat

The horizon is endless and flat
Sickness on seas does not let go
The light you remember, where you once sat
The stillness of death is a tableau

Sickness on seas does not let go
The hopeless delusion: that we could escape
The stillness of death is a tableau
Now we have lost too much, too late

The hopeless delusion: that we could escape
This life at the edge of the world
Now we have lost too much, too late
Waves took our bodies that sheets unfurled

This life at the edge of the world—
Anywhere is closer to home than here.
Waves took our bodies that sheets unfurled
As soon as you leave, your land is near.

St Kilda, Australia

Lady of St Kilda

A bonny, fair thing, that schooner, that boat
Docked from Devon all the way to the ends of the earth
A traveling cargo ship of perishable goods; human, fruit
You name it she took it on board.

The Azores, Spain, Italy, London, the Outer Hebrides
What a swift course she travelled, a fast topsail with
Masts raked high and steep, a curved clipper bow
And a fantail stern like the little Antipodean bird.

Sir Thomas Acland, what a chap! In love with his wife,
Lydia, set sail with their son, little Thomas the younger
To the island of St Kilda to see the strange folk there
And their odd, remote ways. How romantic it was!

For that, he named his boat after his own lady
And the striking island of primitive Gaelic speakers:
Women who sat half naked, hunched over their spinning wheels
Men whose plaids were fastened with the bill of an oyster catcher.

How was it possible? Stripped to their underclothes
To scale the rocks. They say the same peat fire burned for centuries
In St Kilda, not a match to be found anywhere on the island.
How wonderful! To think of life so unchanged.

The ship with its seagoing grace, named in part for love
And in part hysteria, for Lady Grange, who was imprisoned
On St Kilda by her very own husband, the shame!
And then, when the time was right, he let his billowing boat go,

Sir Thomas Acland, there it slipped at a rate of great knots
All the way to Australia. Before he sold his sea bearing
Yacht, his graceful lady, he took one last trip to St Kilda
To bring gifts of fruit and pennies and provisions.

Such generosity, such charity led the St Kildans to flee
Eventually. To see their own poverty, to hate the stench
Of their burnt birds and their slick oils and their sick babies
And their windy climes and impossible rocks and whipping winds.

Off she went, the Lady of St Kilda, Down Under to newly
Mapped territories. She landed by a green knoll and floated
On for listless sunny days that repeated themselves endlessly.
So shiny was Australia—not like that ragged, wretched Scottish coast.

Some say that's how it got its name, the suburb of St Kilda.
LaTrobe was picnicking and saw the handsome ship
Out in the bay, gleaming white sails puffed up like a pelican.
The governor and his family, they decided there and then.

On the railway bridge, outside Balaclava station
There is an artwork of the ship, a cartoon version
In metal, of her rippling sails. I look at it often
When I walk under the rails. And wonder at that boat.

1001 Nights

At Café Scheherazade they're still telling tales
those eternal single men who came over after the war
after everyone they knew was shot or gassed.
They're huddled around the same round table
on Acland Street at the front of the restaurant
the garish 1950s wallpaper adorns them like shirts,
giant golden flowers against a brown backdrop.

They're having the conversation about property
how back in the day an entire apartment building
cost $10,000 and now it's worth $4 million.
If only they had bought then. But who knew?
They shrug, drink black coffee, eat gefilte fish, chopped
chicken liver, latkes and kreplach, slurp borscht
half hunched over, like this is a poker game
and they've already lost.

Outside, skinny pairs of women walk by
in short shorts so short
you can see the scoop of their asses.
They're always going to the beach or coming from it
in their neon colours, their electric smiles.

The men at the table don't even look up.
They talk until the piece of furniture they sit at
floats out to sea; their vessel, their only home.
The hair on their heads the one thing visibly receding,
and the horizon, that too, drifts away.

Crossing Over

I'm staying in a four-bunk room at The Ritz.
The girl on top is an ex-dancer, she talks
in a husky voice about nightclubs and laughs
like a carrion bird.

I am destined to smoke cigarettes
on a fake Juliette balcony we barely fit on
through windows that don't quite open in
spaces too small for travellers to truly
sleep. We are reaching out towards rain,
trying to glide our lives forward
to somewhere ecstatic.

I don't make it outside for days. Just communal
kitchens and overheard conversations with back alley
hookers. And trams that rattle past
and shake all the windows of the tall slender
building that is The Ritz on Fitzroy Street.
A small series of tremors
that might lead to something bigger.

When I do go out it is to a bridge. A spiral
of concrete that connects the Upper Esplanade
to the Lower. It seems impossible to see the sea
but there it is, flat-lining and still.

A view all the way to the horizon all the way
across the bay to the Tasman, to where I've come from.
The flat landscape with only one tanker ship
and a sail boat and the possibility of another day.

Prahran Station

It was there on that train platform
at Prahran station, that I decided
to stay.

Called home to Canada
from a payphone and the train
rattle kept on interrupting

so I could hardly hear what I was saying
or the silence between that
and my mother's response.

"I'm staying in Melbourne."

I think the silence lasted as long
as a train takes to pull into a station
release passengers, take new ones on board

and hurry off, a noisy blur
a jolt, a shake of landscape
and then nothing but the buzz

of electrical wires and the calls of
crested cockatoos or rosy gallahs
who cry out in repetition.

Then my mother at the end of the line:
"Just don't meet someone when you are there,
just don't marry an Australian."

As though this was a cautionary tale
or a moral at the end of a story.

I wanted to tell her about weedy sea dragons
under the water, beautiful and strange.
There are creatures here I cannot begin to fathom.
Instead I lost connection

left with the boom box blare of cars
on Chapel Street and the conference
of girls in school uniform from Wesley

who stop in at the cafés on Greville Street
for a frappé or a green juice or a cappuccino
just like their mothers before them.

They flip their hair, they smile wide
or brood or bitch or giggle
like they are meant to, like teenage clockwork.

And Prahran is such an unusual word.
I assumed it was English, like most things around here,
some appropriated name from the Homeland.

But it's Aboriginal. Two words strung together
and then spelled phonetically.
It means: "Land partially surrounded by water."

St Kilda Pier, 2003

Someone has set fire to the kiosk
the one with the weather vane
the horseshoe arches
the iron roof
the lamingtons
the ice slushies
and the bad coffee.

It sat like a mollusk in its shell
at the end of that long wooden pier:
where the fishermen would wait
at dusk with their white buckets
phosphorescent under lamplight
and moonlight.
Those buckets with the fish guts
and the worms.
Those fishermen from Albania
and Italy and Greece
from Colac and Geelong and Warnambool.

They would sit and fish, as couples
held hands and pretended to love
each other and teenagers drifted
by on skateboards
clack, clack, clack, clack
the clip of wheels against
slats of wood a workman laid down
without nails
a century ago.

And now the kiosk at the end
of St Kilda pier is on fire

the one that was built in 1903
run by a family who served
"fish and fruit luncheons
without any intoxicating liquors
of any sort!"
Then by a man who kept
sheep in a shed behind the kiosk
busied himself saving lives,
just jumped in the water and rescued
500 people over 49 years.

When I arrived in St Kilda
I went first to that pier
I went to water
because geographically that helped me
to know where I was.

It seemed like there was no one there
that day, just the sky.
Like the whole place had cleared out
so I could feel even more alone
than I already did.

When it's quiet enough you can hear
the little fairy penguins nesting
in the breakwater.
They're a native species
and they forage here.
The food is good and close
and the structure underneath
is labyrinthine, perfect for nesting.

I, too, want to nest
under a rock and forage
for pilchards and anchovy

in the saltbush grasses
with only a starfish
looking on from below
in the clear water.
A starfish:
It seems impossible.

Golem

A black bowler hat and long black coat—
winter or summer, always the same immaculate
clothes that made no sense. His white hair poking
out in tufts around the rim.

He would walk the beach, gather up litter
or look for treasure like his eyes were
metal detectors, his hand a magnet.

I would come across him on Acland street, the leafy end
near the Alliance Française, the breezy cafes,
the art gallery in the old converted house
with a courtyard: the end that tried to stay sane.

He would wander there, his presence
like one of the tzadikim, a testament to
the impossible. Muttering in Yiddish, I think
or a language he had made up, a gibberish
reserved for highly skilled clowns.

Across from my seat on the 96 tram
he would often sit, like I had dreamed him there.
He would weave back together the threads
that had come unravelled in his pocket.

A long black woolen line tracing to Poland
to history and war, to memory, all with the stroke
of his fingers, kneading time.
I tried not to look, just sit with
the collection of him.

Like I might absorb something. Wisdom in
the madness of sunlight flying through a tram
lined with ads for health insurance
and holidays and how to be happier sooner.

I would close my eyes between stops.
And when I opened them
he'd disappear. A hole in time
he tumbled through, no doubt.

Love Story

We said things over soy lattes.
Life was so mundane and comfortable
it was murder to live like that
and not even know it.

Your place was right by the Jewish Museum
on Alma Road. Soul Road.
The rooms were haunted with bad spirits
and smelled like your ex.
No, worse than that. It *was* her place
you just took it over
like some kind of mamma's boy.
I was in love with you
but you didn't have a mind of your own
and that scared me.

Once, I climbed through your kitchen window,
to be with you.
I got pierced by the rosebushes outside.
That's love, right?
Risking it all like that.

At the café right by your house
we used to wait for the boat table—
the one that stuck out in a triangle of planks.
It was uncomfortable to sit at
but so perfect and intimate
we always wanted to shove our legs
under it and crunch up.
Because at that point we weren't going out
we were just rubbing knees
and pretending to be best friends.

It was around then I started lying.
Because I loved you, but couldn't love you.
And since I was on the other
side of the world no one knew me well enough
to tell me that I had become a liar.
You saw it, but were in on the lie.
Because you loved me, but couldn't love me.

We were pinned like that.
It felt like a whole lifetime passed,
a lost decade at that boat table in St Kilda.
I'm telling the truth now.
It hurts to tell the truth,
like pulling a fish hook
out of your palette.

Streets Named after Poets

We lived on Mason Avenue, the only street
in the area not named after a poet.

There was Milton and Byron, Wordsworth
and Tennyson, Shelley and Keats.

11 Mason Avenue—the street named after a cult—had
a blue door and frangipani out the front.

Our neighbours were Buddhists.
When you poked your head over the fence

to say hello, there were Tibetan Prayer flags
and a painted outhouse and a tended garden.

The prayer flags weren't in tatters,
they were bright and strong, pulled taut

at 13 Mason Avenue, where people
really did pray and Tibetan lamas came to visit.

The neighbourhood used to be a swamp
that flooded all the time.

There was a human manure depot down
the road. In other words: it was a dump.

But that was the 1800s. Now it was desirable
and gentrified, with stately houses and shady streets

lined with plane trees, that made everyone allergic.
Cobblestone drains and dead ends from the canal were all

that was left from the early days. I would often get lost on my way
home, wind up on some street that went nowhere, a footbridge

over a canal. I would ride a blue bicycle through the St Kilda
Botanical Gardens to get to work.

The lorikeets singing in the palm trees
the roses often in bloom and flowers

I could not name. Desert blossoms.
Life was simple for a while.

I worked in a café and made coffee
with leaves or hearts on top.

That was all, just pulled coffee
out of one of those old fashioned Italian machines.

All those beans, all that froth
all those tiny pieces of white paper like prayer flags

with abbreviated messages on them above
the coffee machine: LB and FW and V. Hot Sk. L.

I became close to those neighbours and their daughter
and my two flatmates, who both had the same name.

Years later I had lost touch with them all.
I knew the neighbours lived on top of a mountain now.

I was on a drive from Brisbane back to Sydney
with a theatre set in a trailer hitched to the back of my car.

I lost control. Overcorrected the steering on a corner.
That trailer swung back and forth like a crazy pendulum

finally took me with it, spun a full 360
and fell off the side of the road upside down

in a paddock full of mud and shit.
It was probably the wet cow dung that saved my life.

I crawled out of the passenger seat window, up the hill
where onlookers had pulled over, waiting to see a ghost

waft up from that valley. Time stopped when I fell
through the air, the way it would before you die

that free fall from the chute of life, wind blowing
through my ears, even with the windows closed

a kind of peace knowing there was nothing I could do
in those few seconds before impact.

The last thing I saw before the crash
was a purple Ford Fiesta; my neighbour's car.

It passed me on the other side
of the Pacific Highway and I thought of her.

I didn't know she had died, never learned how.
Just knew she watched that moment before I fell.

I walked out without a scratch. Well, a small piece of glass
embedded in my thumb.

The onlookers wondered about the others, surely someone
had died. No one else was in the car.

Just the stuffing from an old armchair, the springs loose
joggled out and the splinter of wood from the set pieces.

The ear of a donkey puppet folded back.
The cage of the trailer crushed, the car totalled.

I stood in a field, waited for the police to come,
and wondered at the muddied wreck, my luck.

Montreal, Canada

It's Not the Same Now That You're Dead

I can't drive on that side of the mountain now.
By the hospital. The avenue des Pins side.
Not that I drive in this town, anyway. It feels wrong.
There are too many bikes, and people swearing out car windows.
And I learned to drive on the other side of the road.
It makes more sense when the steering wheel
is on the right.

But that's not the point. The point is: it's not the same
now that you're dead. And not just you. Lots of people.
The ones who died and left this town empty.
It's one thing to move away. To say: it's too French,
there aren't enough jobs, there are too many holes in the roads,
what are people doing living this far north, anyway?

It's one thing to say: I can't stand the winters, they're too long,
there's too much snow, who can live like this?
Or to say: I'm moving to Toronto, everyone is moving to Toronto,
it's better in Toronto, I hate Toronto but I'm moving there anyway.

But to up and die and leave this hole, this massive hole?
Bigger than the winter thaw on city streets, bigger
than the chunks of concrete falling off the overpasses,
bigger than the sinkhole that suddenly appeared
on avenue Guy the other day. The one a small truck fell through.
That leaves people feeling bad.

I don't even know where to begin to look for all of you,
the ones who died and left this place empty.
They are too many holes in the infrastructure in Montreal,
apparently. And now we are starting to feel it.
I'm starting to feel it.

Runt

So small I could fit in a seashell,
a pea pod.
A little nothing
an unborn thing.

I fade into the background
of photographs
short hair, boyish,
you can't tell
what sex
I am.

A pipsqueak
a marble you roll
around in your mouth.
I blur when you look at me
I don't have breasts yet
I don't have my period.

In the girl's bathroom they talk
about lesbian kissing,
how they lost it
to a boy at a party last week
while everyone was watching.

I don't even go to parties
I sing in choirs
I suck my thumb at night sometimes
I hold onto a stuffed animal in the dark.
I kiss Rob Lowe posters for practice
I kiss the pillow, smother my face
in its embrace
suffocate there a moment.

Silent scream
into a tiny oblivion.
I'm that speck
at the edge of your vision.
See me disappear.

Stalking Christopher Reeve

I guess they were making *Superman*, or a sequel
to something. What did we know?

Squealing girls, ponytails tied high behind us.
We tramped the downtown streets
like we owned them.

That shortcut by the school we always took that weaved
around the red brick church, chain fences surrounding
the concrete yard we had just escaped.

The fancy apartment building with the awning
on Milton across from the pizza place
was where he was staying, apparently.

"Christopher Reeve, come out of there!"
We shouted at shut windows
hoped that the doorman would notice us

take us away screaming down the street until
Christopher would come out and say:
"No, no, they're OK. They're my fans."

And then later he fell on his head
and broke his neck.
We had gotten over him by then, but still.

It hurt to think of it.
The way a high up place hurts from vertigo.
How something falling from a height—

a penny, a body,
even just in your mind—hits hard.

Grey Gardens

We would sit on your bed and watch, stoned.
I never got stoned except with you
with anyone else it made me feel sick
with you it made me feel more alive.
A little queasy and the world blurred, sure
but everything was like a roller coaster with you.

I had this terrible crush. I told you about it
you laughed. Told me you were gay
I withdrew the knife from my wrist
that was poised so delicately there and promised
never to kill myself over you then.
Unrequited love in this case didn't count.

We hung out a lot after that. Did a lot of drugs.
Life was better when I was in your company
—more vivid
you seemed to be some kind of great wave
of everything that mattered.
But that was only when I was with you

apart, I felt a bit bland. And that seemed unfair
for you to hold all that.
So I would only see you sometimes
Most of the time I just tried to live my life.

Grey Gardens was horrible. About decay
and the human condition
about this terrible kind of love between a mother
and daughter. They even had the same name.

It was so creepy.
You watched it a lot, over and over.
Stoned.
Which was kind of weird.

And then I would sleep over,
you spooning me in our pyjamas
like some kind of incestuous
brother and sister pair from a fairy tale.

The Good Years

We tugged on electrical wires for fun, just to see
if we could get a shock.

And when I say we, I mean teenagers
who have no idea what to do with an afternoon.

And when I say teenagers, I mean a bunch of anorexic
layabouts who are deeply depressed, highly sexually charged

and strangely gleeful, as though we were all harbouring
fireflies inside our hearts.

We gave each other bunches of things: fistfuls of hair
we had pulled out, heads off flowers we had yanked

while walking down the old alleyways we used,
bits of scrap paper with nothing significant on them.

We rarely spoke of how puking was making our teeth rot
or how growing up seemed to be a very bad idea

and dying first was definitely better. One of us, the tall one,
the skinniest one, saw a dead rat once.

It stank and it was stiff and it broke her heart—
shattered it and let the fireflies out and set the world alight.

And she felt hungry again, starting with apples but soon moving on to crêpes.
We forgot to starve ourselves and our teeth got less loose in our mouths

and we smiled more, even if we were dying anyway.
We smiled more, and we weren't in such a hurry.

The Rapture of 1989

They say it is coming and when it does
even Ronald Regan will lose his cool.
The streets will be set alight
with how bright it all is.
The second coming, and all.

And we will no doubt float away
on clouds of ecstatic
revelry, wearing head bands
made of terry cloth and sweat suits
our mothers sewed themselves.

We grew up in the seventies
and the angels were always
going to arrive
in stardust and bell bottoms
trailed by hazy music—
something faintly familiar
and cringe worthy.

Hopefully not death metal
because that would really
be a disappointment
if it ended that way after all.

Polaroid

I am on the swing set
beside my sister—sitting, not swinging.
We look like morose angels
despite my yellow sundress
with the eyelets and the flared sleeves
cut out like petals around the edges,
high waist hugging into
my ribs.

My sister wears a dress so wildy
patterned it pins us to the 1970s,
but the white Polaroid edges
can barely contain us in the frame.

My father is behind the lens,
one foot already out the door.
That was before the summer
of the hornet's nest. Before he
disappeared entirely

and a swarm moved in,
perched over the threshold
so that we could no longer
enter without uncertainty.

I don't remember if my mother
called an exterminator
or if the nest loosened itself
from the bricks above the front
door of the house.

It lay on our doorstep,
a papery corpse
I was afraid to touch
in case the powdery shell
release a thousand
furious bodies.

Or worse, collapse
under my fingers
and what was left of all that life
spill out at my feet.

Benny Pool With My Sister, 1981

Children look so quizzical and v-neck
bathing suits are all the rage. Tri-tone
tops on flat-chested youth are
all, all wasted anyway.

We do this every summer, this back
and forth from the public pool. Bored
with the ache of our days, not one thing
to look forward to but water.

You look at me in the car as though you want
to know the answer to every question
in 1981 and beyond.

I wish I had something to give you.
Something to bless
you with. A benediction.
The truth.

I wish I could have said; *You won't want to
commit suicide, our parents will be together
forever, your pet parakeet will come back, no one
here dies.*

If only I had it in me to be a liar.
But when I swim
I see things, fragments
that add up to the future.

My Grandfather, the Barber, Speaks from the Dead

If I had known that cutting hair would be so useful
I would have taught you.

In the afterlife, your hair keeps growing.
Just like in the war.

They've got me working as a barber here too,
no heavy labour for me

no cutting down trees in Siberia. Hair tonic:
it made me popular with the Russians.

My advice to you: get a skill. All that reading
you're doing, when you're dead, it will get you nowhere.

And the writing, well, that might come in
handy. But I doubt it.

The Book has already been written, if
you know what I mean.

It's possible we all create our own heaven
and hell. Mine is

a barber shop with a revolving door: the customers
just keep coming.

It's all the same, you know. As above
so below.

Ice Storm, 1998

The day I say goodbye
pylons collapse. Tunnels close. Bridges shut.
I never meant to leave quite like this.

I climb on a train.
The tracks I leave behind are slicked,
glistening with slippery impossibility.
No way back to the island now.

The minute I arrive in New York I call my mother
my father, my grandmother, my sister, my aunt:
*"Due to a high volume of calls to this area we are
unable to complete your request at this time."*

I never meant to leave quite like this.
Pavement fractures, utility poles snap,
a thousand trees give under the weight.

When I stop in California, we sit round the television,
watch basketball, flip channels to see
what's going on in Montreal.
My friend is from there too, we both regret

not being home. The winters we survived
and now we're missing this!
Everyone says we're crazy
to pine for a disaster.

We want to be under ice,
under house arrest.
We want to watch the army clear the streets
of the shattered debris. Huddle by generator power.
We want to be able to say: we were there.

I finally arrive in Australia.
I traded it all for a platypus I saw
slipping through a rare cool stream.
They are reclusive creatures, difficult to spot.

This is Home

"And they don't run very quickly because they're diving birds"
The Cape Breton Post, December 20, 2011

From above, Crescent Street
was a slippery black tarmac,
a landing strip complete
with flashing lights.

Sex unknown, friendless
the puffin waddled and weaved
in and out of traffic.
Until a veterinary technician
(who happened to be passing by)
scooped the fledgling up
and transferred it
to a bathtub bunker.

The bird had hitched a ride on a barge
down the St Lawrence, no doubt.
A not yet one-year-old runaway
with big dreams. City aspirations.
All that gulping of fish.
All that huddling on rocks.
All that frigid water.
Something had to give.

Through the generations
of Grand Banks puffins,
someone had to set their sights higher.
A puffin after a linguistic challenge
and culinary variety.
A bird after a cold beer on Crescent Street,

although St Laurent might have been
a better choice to a native.

But dreams don't last long.
The bathtub bunker is slick white
a hollow to waddle in
while two daily meals of cut smelt
and vitamins are delivered
straight down the gullet.

Not half bad really
considering all that diving
that normally goes on,
face first in the frigid sea
lucky if you catch anything at all.

Now they say they're trying to get
the bird back home to St John's
for Christmas.
Most of the puffins have already migrated
so this straggler is going to be tricky
to place.

No one wants to pay
the wayward orphan's ticket
to an outcrop of rocks unnamed
somewhere off Ship Cove
in Placentia Bay.

And Placentia makes me think of placenta,
makes me think of things that grow
inside other things.
But you are a bird and hatched from an egg.
For all we know your family walked away
glided across a body of water, left you

to feed off rejected fish heads and entrails
gulp beakfulls of sea until you knew better.
For all we know, you were abandoned.

You do get home for Christmas.
Courtesy of Air Canada,
flown in a hammock bed inside a crate.
Your passage was announced on the flight:
"The puffin is on board."
The Canadian Coast Guard kindly dropped
you off. It was a national effort.

They found a small colony
who hadn't migrated yet,
birds who turned their beaks
towards the bitter air,
toughed it out for a while.

It was a success story
by all human standards.
We returned you home.
You're home, right?
This is home.

Santorini, Greece

I had a cypress tree in my house
I had a cypress tree in my room.
The North wind blew
It toppled the cypress tree,
And I lost my pillar of strength.

–Traditional Greek Funeral Liturgy

Under This Soft Earth Lies a Buried City 3600 Years Old

The first thing you see when you reach the island is white light from the rounded buildings. At first every house looks the same and the churches are distinguishable only by the stone crosses on the rooftops. You have no sense of direction here, and no map can guide you. For the first time in your life you are totally alone. The entrance to the city is a gate to a graveyard. Inside, people are buried under white rectangular tombs. Water candles flicker on top of gravestones, and the faces of the dead rest in photographs beneath glass, a small shrine to remind the living to stay alive. The moon is a new crescent tonight; on the black water-surface it swims a sideways smile. It is a reflection of the shape this island has become. Just as this island was once a full circle, so too was the moon once fat and round. The island is still waning, falling stone by stone into the sea. Do not try and find your way, you will only get lost. Do not give up looking, or the light will go out. Do not reconcile yourself to the hopelessness of your situation, or you will be defeated. Look neither up nor down, neither straight ahead nor behind you. Imagine you have eyes all over your body. It is not your responsibility to choose which ones to see out of.

Cavehouse

Yesterday I met a man who brought me to a cave. He said he could read people's dreams. He said I was meant to stay here. He said he nearly died from spilling hot marble all over his body. He said he read coffee grounds. He asked me my name. He said in Greek it was the name of a muse. He led me through a labyrinth, a twisting village all in white with only one yellow house. He took me to a cave, this cave, and said I could stay. He said I had to tend his animals and otherwise I was free to live here until he returned. He did not say when he would return. He gave me a key to the front door. He showed me the door to the cave and I laughed and said caves do not have doors. This cave has doors. Three doors. I only have one key, to the first door. He said a man would come the next day and show me what I must do. He did not speak a word of English. I do not speak a word of Greek. He spoke in gestures and in words which sounded like a language I understood, although I knew I had never heard it before. He made tea out of purple flowers in a black Japanese pot. The tea was magenta, an impossible colour. It tasted like a memory I could not place. I let the flowers sink to the bottom and cradled the rounded cup that had no handles. We sat at a table on low benches covered in coarse animal-hair rugs. We sat until the tea turned deep purple. I wondered if he could read tea-leaves. He left before I could ask him anything; his name, when he would return, why he had chosen me, a stranger, to take care of his house and his donkey. I am alone in a cave which is a house. When I close my eyes I can feel what it is to be in the earth. This is where I will begin.

How To

The painter—named after a constellation—shows me things. He shows me how to get water from a well, at what angle the bucket has to fall and how much force I have to use to pull it up so that it is full. "Never let go of the rope," he says. He shows me how to cook an enormous pot of rice and how much meat to add when it is done. He shows me how much milk to mix the rice with for the cats. He shows me where the sacks of rice are kept and where the boxes of canned milk are stored. He gives me the key to a room filled with hay, which is next to the yellow house. He shows me how to throw hay so that it lands in the donkey's patch. "The donkey is wild but do not be afraid," he says. He shows me how I must fill pails of water for her and carry them down into the field without spilling any. He shows me how to turn on the gas burners in the house and what to do when the gas runs out. He tells me how often to feed the animals and shows me how much. He shows me all the herbs in the garden and what needs to be watered. He points towards a path and tells me it leads to the sea. He points towards a road barely visible from here and shows me the direction he lives in. He says he will be back in one week to be sure I am alright. On his way down the stone steps to the donkey path, he says: "This is how you will live."

Morning Light

I dream of elephants, of Minoan men exchanging tusks and offering them to the gods. When I wake up I am in a cave. The walls are round and coarse and painted white. Small arched windows are carved into the walls as shelves. They do not look out onto anything except the earth they are made of. On all of the ledges there are glass bottles, stones and pieces of uncarved wood. An incense burner, like the one a priest would hold, sits on an unfinished wood table. A divan covered with a Turkish carpet is pushed against one wall, and the bed I am lying on rests on a white concrete rectangular frame. It looks like the graves I have seen here, which sit above ground. There is a small window over the cave door which is covered with a spiralled iron grating. The curved metal makes a shadow on the wall. I trace its pattern in my mind; the circular shape chasing its own tail, turning in upon itself. This is the only source of light, a thin spiral stream which seems to come from nowhere. It is hard to imagine that there is a sun outside, or a garden full of morning light, with flowers opening their heads and bees humming in the oregano.

Ghost Eyes

The sea wails under the cave entrance at night. I wait for it to rush in while I am sleeping. The old dog scratches at the floor in the dark, as if he were digging up a garden. His yellow nails scrape and brush the linoleum in frantic rhythms, syncopating the swells of the sea. I hear ghosts in the front room, dancing the circumference of the kitchen table, taking refuge from the rain. I don't dare to open my eyes. There will be eyes looking back at me. The gaze of the dead hangs about the room, shifting like stones in a crumbling wall. I feel the weight of centuries pressing against me. I feel the form of this cave changing. As soon as I close my eyes the metamorphosis begins. The air around me fills with the soft rustle of insect wings. The rose-petal skin of moths tickles my eyelids. Animal tails tangle in my hair. Dead hands hold me above the bed. I can't lie down without the sensation of being lifted and suspended. Perhaps it is this darkness, the black blindness of this burrow, which fills me with visions. Or is it the silence that stirs me to such an intent listening? I can hear my breath as a great wind across the prairie quiet. When there is a storm on the sea I can hear the water lapping at my door. In the morning I expect to be floating, my bed a life-raft on an endless swell of salt-water.

Donkey Paths

Children climb my legs as if they were staircases leading somewhere. "Take me with you," they demand. As if I were going on a journey, as if I had a map in my back pocket, or small change even. No, I only have these pieces of paper ripped down the middle in this pocket with loose threads along the seam. And this paper holds nothing, not even lines which could be translated into roads. No, these are not roads; these are donkey paths. There are no addresses here; only signs that indicate where one might live. There, up there, that white house on the left. The one next to the yellow dome, ten meters from the church no one goes to anymore. The one that has not been whitewashed for a while. The walls are peeling, but paint is expensive these days, and the rain will wash it away eventually, and the walls will collapse eventually, and this island will reclaim itself eventually and there will only be donkey paths and no small bells will ring, because that will be the day the donkeys own this island and nothing will hang around their necks.

Horse Tails

I tell the island children that I have a horse in my back pocket. They have never seen a horse before. Everything moves too slowly here for anything but the twitching donkey. "I have a horse in my back pocket, you can hear him when I walk—Listen carefully— Can you hear him? You're not listening. There. Did you hear? Close your eyes, you'll hear." And I will be gone as fast as that horse who lives in my pocket can carry me. There is a rip in the seam where he can escape and once he is out I jump on his back and we go. Faster than the donkey's tail can fight off flies. Faster than children can open their eyes and see that I am gone. "We hear," they say. But no one answers.

The Language of Donkeys

Stavros still ploughs his fields with a donkey. They move around his circumference of land, getting the soil ready for sowing. With a short reed for a prod he hits the donkey on the side of the head and occasionally kicks her in the belly. He speaks a donkey language. It is an acquired tongue that the island riders have refined over the years. They speak it to their wives at night. It is a series of grunts with different pitches and intonations which take on the rhythm of language: "Faster" "Slower" "Stay left" "Stop" "I'll leave you here for the night." Only the donkeys and their riders understand. Their secret language echoes through the steep village paths along with the hollow sound of donkey hooves. The farmer's wives crawl into bed at night puzzled by the beasts they live with. In the early morning men ride in a row on donkey back, shouting incomprehensibly, as if they were trying to start a revolution. Their wives stay at home; sweeping the stoop, sweeping the stoop, they could make concrete bleed with all that sweeping. Those women have taken to talking to themselves, muttering under their breath and singing: "Yassou, Yassou," like trained birds when someone walks by.

There are Eyes All Over This Island

The red eyes of dogs who guard the graveyard and have no owners, the black eyes of donkeys who stay tethered in a rocky field all night blinking with the night's breath. The eyes in the photographs of the dead, which seem to move as the light moves. The eyes of the sleeping which remain shut even though your stranger's footsteps echo through the city. The eyes of swallows and nightingales looking over the island, as they dart along the fringe but never land on these shores. The eyes of fish looking sideways through water, judging each step you take by the soft pumice your feet unsettle down the cliff face, falling on them like rain. The eyes of an octopus searching for a deeper place to hide from the nets that are cast in early morning. There are the eyes of fishermen who sleep with one eye open, monitoring the light's progression towards dawn. There are the blind eyes of snails, groping and edging their way up stone walls. There are the eyes of lizards squinting and opening in the sun like signs trying to tell you something. There are your eyes as well; your foreign, seeking eyes, looking for a place to spend the night, a road that does not echo solitude, a path that does not lead through graveyards. You do not belong here, but now that your boat has come upon these shores and you have climbed the five hundred steps up the cliff-face to ground you can stand on, you have to stay. This island is calling your name.

Snail's Pace

Snails curl their way up stonewalls, spiralling like inner ears. They are listening to the sounds I cannot hear. If I put my ear to the earth, could I find the same rhythm of silence as the creeping snails? Their crustaceous backs are imprinted with the patterns of time, written in an indelible language. Each marking contains a question and answer within its own unsolvable mystery. I watch the slow progress of snails. Their sticky bodies pressed against cold stone. Each groove in the wall is an indication of what is to come, a place to hold onto. I take my own finger for a walk alongside the groping creatures. They send out pointed feelers in my direction. I am an obstacle in their path. Blind, they know what stands in their way. Without limbs they move forward, grabbing at a destination. The movement of snails is a dance in slow motion, a perfect co-ordination of time and space. I inch my way down donkey paths, each footstep suctioned to the earth. I close my eyes and feel what it is to stand on solid ground. My skin holds a pattern, a blueprint of my life. I wear it like a song. I listen to the music of my skin, the history of my cells, the sorrow of my blood. I follow the maps of my veins, the explosions of light my atoms make as electrons fall towards the nucleus. I move as slowly as a snail, going nowhere, always arriving.

We are the Bones We Walk On

Under the white sand I stand on, there lies the evaporated bodies of crabs, the empty shells of oysters, the spiny casings of sea urchins, the finger-like remains of fish, the prehistoric bones of small elephants who once walked here before anything but the beating heart kept track of life passing. The head of a donkey, its bottom jaw separated from the skull, yawns on the beach. Under the sea, the vertebrae of dolphins are staircases connecting the underworld to water. These paths I walk on are made of ground bone. Mortar and pestle feet walked here and crushed the insides of donkeys into a pale brown dust, fine and soft. Each layer of the ground holds hundreds of secrets, bone upon bone of what once walked. Each layer of sediment tells a different story: A fisherman who was drowned and washed ashore, buried with the wooden boards of his boat, a two-thousand-year-old woman who formed clay urns in her hands, the fall of a donkey with too many bricks on her back, her over-laden body sliding down the steep path, crushed by her own weight. We are all buried here. This island was once a circle; a beginning, a middle and an end, indistinguishable.

The Story of Bones

The archaeologist's daughter grew up in tombs. She spent her early childhood crawling through the volcanic ash, which preserved time. Her father dug tunnels in the ground, uncovered death masks, stumbled upon bones of winged beasts, while her baby hands clutched the cold earth. The archaeologist supplied his daughter with a trowel and instructed her to dig. Together they set out to uncover all that lay underneath. She was well accustomed to palaces, with their fallen throne rooms, the shards of pottery and frescoes lying in thousands of pieces, the lost gaze of court ladies re-emerging from the fine dust of centuries. She knew the glint of gold teeth poking out after days of discovering nothing but earthworms and the eyes of insects. Her father often buried treasures in her path, artefacts he had already delighted in. She would dig up a bronze spoon that he had just dusted off and buried again. In her eagerness she would run to her father, curling the bones of her hand over a spoon, which had not been held for hundreds of centuries. At night, they would sit under the stars, telling tales about the lives of kings and emperors, queens and courtiers, fools and devils, women and slaves, peasants and lords. It is the archaeologist's job to read bones; to find details in decay, to know what food this jaw ground, to know whose lips this hollow mouth kissed, to know the height of this body from a single remaining femur, to know how long this man lived from the look of his empty eye sockets. Here, on this island, under the midnight sky, the archaeologist and his daughter sit under the canopy of a tent they have erected next to the hole in the ground where a donkey fell through the earth and revealed a city full of stories.

Offerings

Two cypress trees grow in the graveyard. They look like old men bending towards the earth. One whispers his burden to the other, "What can we do?" He asks. "Nothing," replies the other, "there is nothing to be done." They watch over the graveyard with dark green eyes. Their wives come to them in the noonday sun, dressed in black from their heads to their feet. The women sit under the shade of their husbands' enormous bodies. All the while they cry softly, the one saying to the other: "What can we do?" The second widow replying, "Nothing, there is nothing to be done." They light olive oil candles, placing the lanterns in their husbands' hands. They bake bread and rice pudding, offering it to the dead, feeding it to the birds that nest in the old men's arms.

Return

Here is your wine-dark sea. Here is your leather bag that contains the winds. Here is your mountain that touches the gods. Here is your cave that contains the future. Here is your string that holds everything together. Here is your chain for the dogs of chaos. Here is your jar of winged souls. Here is your chariot that drives the sun. Here is your ship that was lost for ten years. Here is the eye from the forehead of the one-eyed devourer. Here is your bow and arrow to prove your identity. Here is the horn from the dancing devil. Here is the story you have been meaning to tell. Here is the hero you wanted to be. Here is the island you had all along. Here is the shore you returned to without knowing you had ever left. When you accept all you have, you will realise who you are.

ACKNOWLEDGEMENTS

Versions of these poems appeared first in *Hazlitt, Grain* and the *2011 Global Anthology*. A selection of the Greek poems won the Bronwen Wallace Award.

Thanks to Wyn Cooper, Natasha Herman, Susan Musgrave, William Weaver, the UBC Department of Creative Writing, The Lockup Writers in Residence Program, the Hunter Writers Centre and Katharine Gillett, the Writers' Trust of Canada and my editor Carmine Starnino.

Several books and articles were consulted in the research and writing of this book. In particular: *A Voyage to St Kilda* (Martin, Martin, 1698); *The History of St Kilda* (Kenneth Maccaulay 1764), *St Kilda Past and Present* (George Seton 1878); *St Kilda* (J. Norman Heathcote, 1900); *St Kilda and Its Birds* (Joseph Wiglesworth, 1903); *Who Killed The Great Auk* (Jeremy Gaskell, 2000); *Feasting, Fowling and Feathers: A History of the Exploitation of Wild Birds* (Michael Shrubb, 2013); "St Kilda and Australia: Emigrants at Peril, 1852-53" (*The Scottish Historical Review;* Eric Richards, Oct. 1992); *The History of St Kilda: from its first Settlement to a City and after, 1840-1930,* Volumes I and II (John Butler Cooper, The St Kilda Historical Association, Australia); *The Show Goes On: The History of St Kilda, 1930 to July 1983,* Volume III, (Anne Longmire, The St Kilda Historical Association, Australia); *Flood Fire and Fever: A History of Elwood* (Meyer Eidelson, The St Kilda Historical Association, Australia), *Thera: Pompei of the Ancient Aegean—Excavations at Akrotiri 1967-1979,* (Christos G. Doumas, 1983); *Unearthing Atlantis* (Charles Pellegrino, 1991).

Signal
EDITIONS

Carmine Starnino, Editor
Michael Harris, Founding Editor